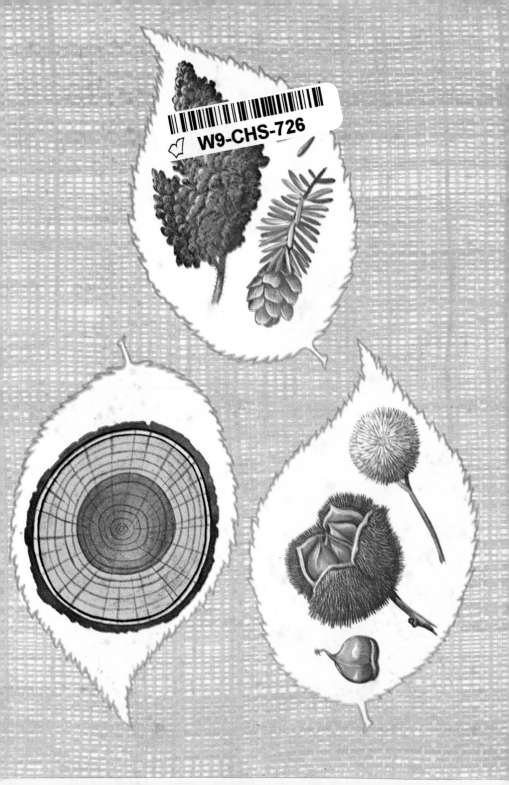

TREES
and How They Grow

by Katharine Carter
illustrated by Valerie Swenson

Prepared under the editorial direction of
Dr. J. F. Stauffer, Professor of Botany,
The University of Wisconsin.

WHITMAN PUBLISHING COMPANY
Racine, Wisconsin

Contents

Library of Congress Catalog Card Number: 61-9976

Printed in the U.S.A.

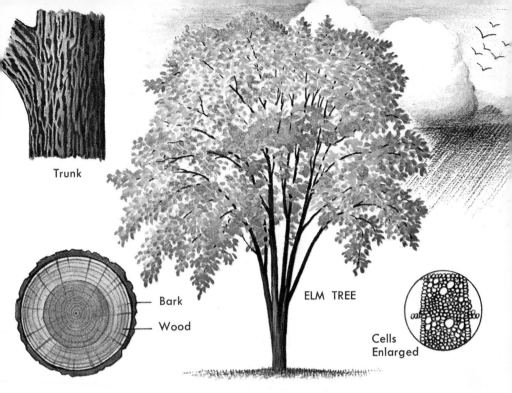

Trunk

Bark

Wood

ELM TREE

Cells
Enlarged

The Miracle of Trees

IN ALL THE SECRETS OF LIFE nothing is more amazing than
the miracles performed by trees. They are the oldest and
largest of all living plants and have many things in common with man. The tree trunk acts much like our bodies,
the bark protecting it as our skin does us. A tree has wood
where we have a spine. Under the outer bark of the trunk
and branches is a thin layer of living cells. These tiny cells
and those in the leaves need oxygen and food as do the
cells of our bodies. And both trees and humans must have
water and air in order to live.

9

Roots

THE ROOTS PLAY A MOST IMPORTANT PART in the life and growth of a tree. They serve as an anchor, holding the tree in place against strong winds. Large trees such as oaks have thousands of roots that go deep into the earth and spread out as wide as do their branches. Their *taproot* is their biggest root, growing straight down with many smaller roots sprouting from it. Other trees have small roots that grow just below the surface.

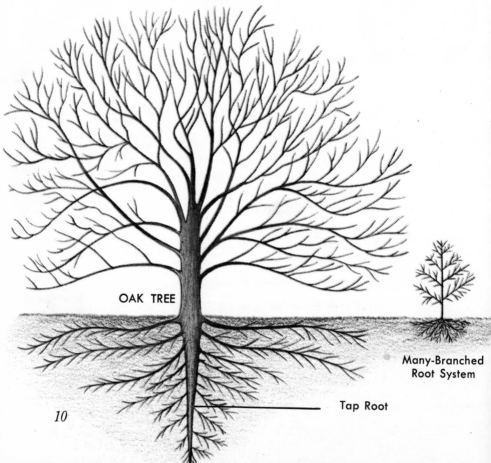

OAK TREE

Many-Branched Root System

Tap Root

Trees that grow among rocks have roots that wind through the cracks.

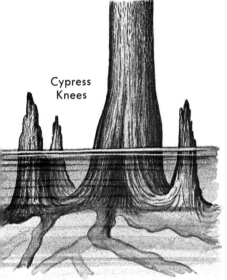

Cypress Knees

The roots of the bald cypress, which grows in damp places, often have outgrowths called knees which rise above the soil or water.

Under a big tree there are millions of small *rootlets*. The tips of these roots are made of cells which grow and divide. Some of them come off and die, forming a protective covering for the root tip. Some of the new cells stay in the root, helping it grow thicker and longer.

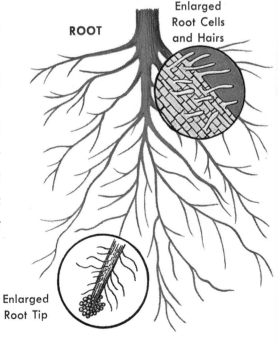

ROOT

Enlarged Root Cells and Hairs

Enlarged Root Tip

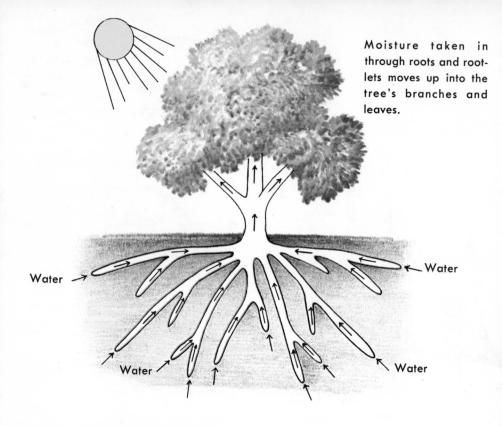

Moisture taken in through roots and root-lets moves up into the tree's branches and leaves.

Water

Water

Water

Water

These rootlets take in moisture from the ground. They pass it on into the older parts of the roots and up through the trunk. From the trunk the moisture is sent into the branches, leaves, and buds. The moisture contains minerals which the tree uses together with the food it makes in the leaves. The food is used to build new bark, wood, leaves, flowers, fruit, and seeds.

Roots also serve as a storehouse for food in winter. The food will be used the next spring when the tree begins to grow again.

Trunk

THE TRUNK IS MADE of many layers. The rough *bark* on the outside is a protective covering. Next to it is an inner bark. Inside that is a thin, white layer called *cambium*. The cambium is the main growing part of the tree. It builds another layer of bark on its outside every year and a layer of wood inside. The new-formed wood becomes part of the *sapwood*. This part contains tubes through which water travels from the roots to the leaves. Every year one or more of the oldest rings of sapwood becomes *heartwood* when the tiny tubes close in autumn. As the tree grows older, the heartwood in the center of the trunk becomes thicker. The age of a cut tree can be found by counting the rings in the sap wood and heartwood.

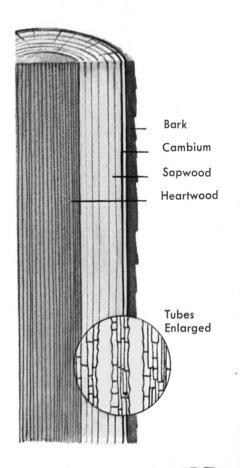

Bark
Cambium
Sapwood
Heartwood

Tubes
Enlarged

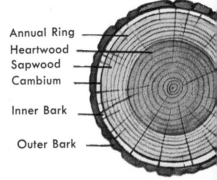

Annual Ring
Heartwood
Sapwood
Cambium

Inner Bark

Outer Bark

Bark

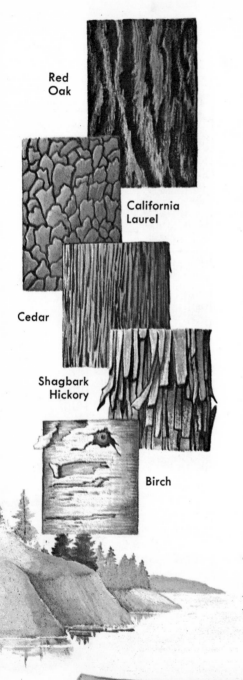

Red Oak

California Laurel

Cedar

Shagbark Hickory

Birch

As a trunk grows in diameter, its outer bark becomes tight. At last it breaks into sections, or splits into strips. These sections stay on the tree and the furrows deepen as the bark becomes thicker. The southern red oak has dark brown bark with deep, narrow ridges. California laurel has smooth, gray-brown bark, which becomes scaly when old.

Some trees have bark that stretches, then peels off. Old cedars often lose their stringy outer bark, leaving the shiny inner layer. The shagbark hickory is correctly named. Its bark peels into shaggy strips, loose at each end, the middle of the strips remaining fastened to the trunk. The bark of the birch can be peeled off in strips. The Indians used these strips to build canoes.

This is how leaves make food. Carbon dioxide enters the leaves and combines with water to form food. Oxygen is given off by the leaves.

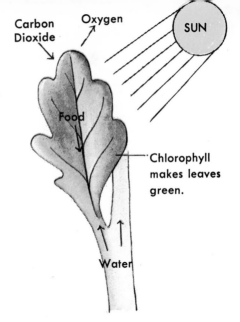

This enlarged section of a leaf shows how air enters the leaf cells.

Chlorophyll makes leaves green.

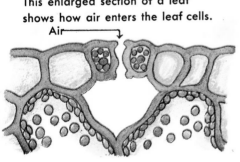

The Work of the Leaves

THE GREATEST MIRACLE performed by trees is that done by the leaves. This marvel nature has given all plants is known as *photosynthesis,* one of the most important processes in our whole existence.

Carbon dioxide from the air moves into the leaves through their tiny pores. The leaves also contain *chlorophyll,* a green pigment which helps the trees perform their food-making miracle. The chlorophyll soaks up the sunlight and the trapped energy is used to combine the carbon dioxide from the air and the water from the roots into sugar, a food. Oxygen is formed at the same time and it moves out of the leaves to become part of the air.

15

Sugar

Sugar

Sugar

Sugar, turned into starch, is stored in the tree's trunk and roots for use when the tree has no leaves to make its food.

The sugar is dissolved by the sap and carried to all parts of the tree as food. When the tree makes more sugar than it needs, the remainder is sent as sap through the cells of the inner bark to the trunk and roots. There the sugar is turned into starch which, in the form of grains, separates from the sap in the cells. Thus the tree can store food for use when it cannot carry on photosynthesis.

Later, as in early spring when the tree begins to grow but has no leaves to make food, this starch is changed back to sugar. This time the sugar moves in the sapwood to the buds and is used to make the cellulose of cell walls. It is also used in making the protein, fats, and many other materials needed by the cells which grow to form leaves, flowers, fruits, and seeds.

The roots of sugar maples send up so much sugar in spring that the sap tastes slightly sweet. Maple syrup is made from it by boiling off most of the water.

In spring the tree's food moves back up into the branches to the growing parts of the tree.

Conifers (Evergreen Trees)

ALL TREES ARE MEMBERS of two general groups or classes. Those that have cones and needlelike leaves belong to the *conifer* group. Their seeds are attached to the upper side of the cone scales and fall out in warm weather. There are about five hundred species, or kinds, of conifers. Pines are the best known.

Many of this group can be recognized by their cones. Sugar pines have the largest cones. They grow from twelve to fifteen or more inches long and take two years to mature. The smallest cones are those of the hemlock—no larger than an acorn. Piñon pines have short, rounded cones with curling scales that make them look like flowers.

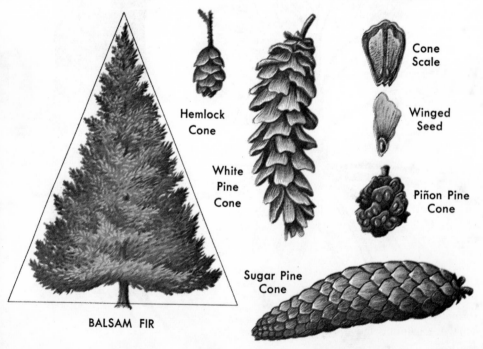

Hemlock Cone

White Pine Cone

Cone Scale

Winged Seed

Piñon Pine Cone

Sugar Pine Cone

BALSAM FIR

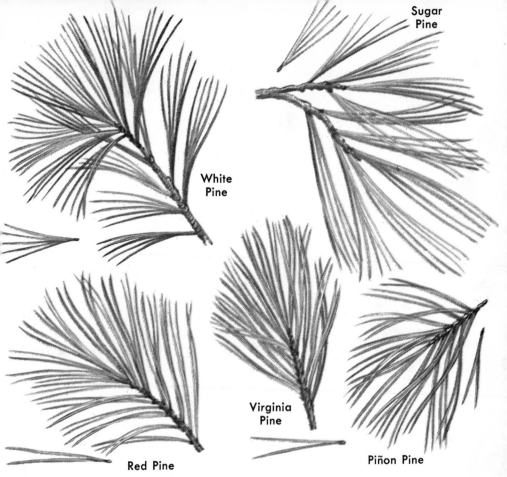

Sugar Pine

White Pine

Virginia Pine

Red Pine

Piñon Pine

Conifers usually have a single trunk, their branches becoming shorter as they near the top, forming a triangular outline. The long, thin leaves of pines grow in groups and look as though they are tied together at the base. Different species of pines can sometimes be partly identified by the number of needles in a cluster. Sugar pines and white pines have five needles in a group. Red pines and Virginia pines have two. Some piñon pines have only one.

Fir Needles

Hair Brush

The leaves, or needles, of spruces and firs are short and stiff. They grow around the twigs in a way similar to bristles on a brush. Cedars have very tiny needles which lie flat against the branches and overlap each other.

Most conifers keep their needles all year and are often called evergreens. But every cone-bearing tree is not necessarily an evergreen. The tamarack has cones, but sheds its leaves in winter.

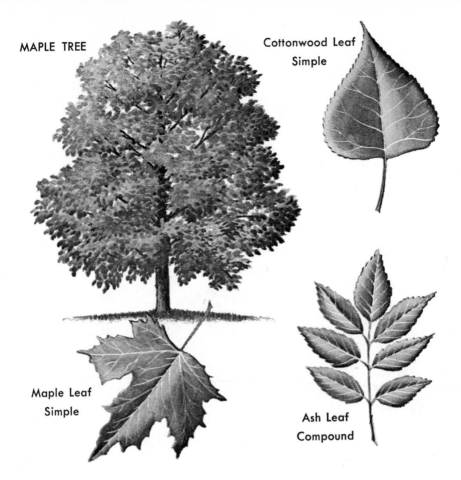

MAPLE TREE

Cottonwood Leaf
Simple

Maple Leaf
Simple

Ash Leaf
Compound

Deciduous (Broadleaf) Trees

Trees with broad leaves such as oaks, maples, and poplars, are members of the *deciduous* group. Their leaves fit into two general types even though they have many shapes. A *simple* leaf is one having a single blade. A leaf with several small leaflets, or blades, growing from each side of the leaf-stem in known as a *compound* leaf.

Deciduous trees lose their leaves in autumn. As the daylight hours become shorter and the nights colder, the work of the leaf cells slows down. A layer of loosely connected cells forms almost completely across the base of each leaf and the sap tubes from the stem into the leaf are closed. This cuts off the leaf's water supply so it dries out and dies. The cells at the base of the stem also shrivel and pull apart, and so the stem breaks and the leaf falls.

As leaves become dry, trees change their colors.

OAK TREE

This dry and brittle leaf is ready to fall.

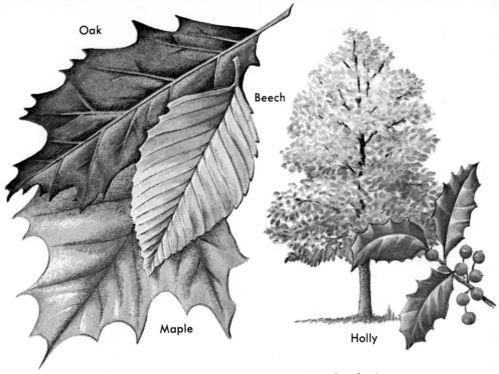

Oak

Beech

Maple

Holly

During the weeks that the leaves are slowly drying out we have the delightful autumn colors. The green chlorophyll disappears, uncovering yellow and orange pigments. In the leaves of some trees the last of the sugar is used to make red pigments. Usually the cells of the leaves also turn brown as they die. These changes lead to many shades of colors. The weather also brings about these changes. A dry autumn causes the leaves to have dull, pale colors, while much rain produces deep, brilliant colors.

There are exceptions in this group, too. The holly is a broadleaf that is evergreen, and so are the live oaks that grow in the South and West.

Palm Trees

THROUGH THE AGES, the regal palm tree has been a blessing to humanity. Of the several kinds, the coconut palms are the most useful. Their oil, nuts, sugar, and leaves are used in thousands of ways. They are grown in southern Florida for decoration and for commercial use. In southern California there are orchards of date palms which supply a large amount of the nutritious fruit.

Palms differ from other trees in that they have no true cambium or heartwood. Their huge fan-shaped leaves are very heavy, some weighing as much as twenty pounds. Desert palms have extremely long roots which push down into the sandy soil to find hidden moisture.

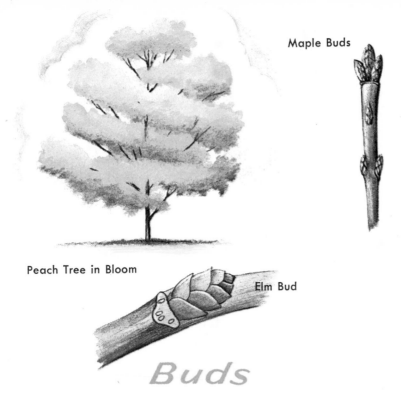

Maple Buds

Peach Tree in Bloom

Elm Bud

Buds

IN WINTER, when the leaves have fallen, it is easy to see the buds on the sides and at the tips of the youngest branches. They were formed the summer before, but now they are resting. These buds contain very young flowers, leaves, or leaves and flowers attached to a little stem. There is also a covering of scale leaves which protects the buds from drying out. During warm spring days the leaves and flowers begin to grow and unfold as if by magic. Each kind of tree has its own bud style.

Maples have three buds at the end of the twigs—a large one in the middle and a small one on each side.

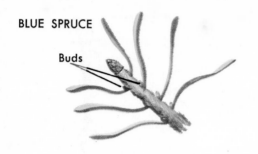

BLUE SPRUCE

Buds

The buds of the blue spruce are almost hidden by the needles. In spring, bunches of green needles push out at the tips of the branches.

Some trees have one kind of bud for their leaves and another for their flowers. Dogwoods have a thin, pointed, red leaf bud. The flower bud is gray, flat underneath and rounded on top, and grows at the end of the twigs.

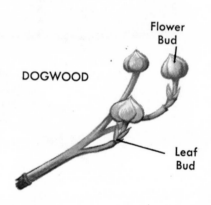

Flower
Bud

DOGWOOD

Leaf
Bud

ELM

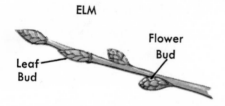

Leaf
Bud

Flower
Bud

Elm flowers are stored in plump, buttonlike buds, while the leaves come from thin, pointed buds.

The cottonwood's leaf buds are at the tips of the twigs and the buds at the sides bear the flowers

26

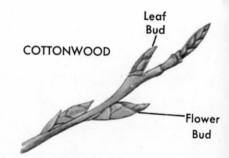

Leaf
Bud

COTTONWOOD

Flower
Bud

From Pollen, More Trees

TREES PRODUCE SEEDS from which new trees may grow. Part of the process of seed production is the transfer of *pollen* from the male part of the flower to the female part. The male part is called the *stamen* and the female part is called the *pistil*.

Pollen looks like tiny yellow grains. It is easily carried by the wind or by insects. Each flower produces thousands of pollen grains and every kind of plant shapes its grains differently. Under a microscope they look like baseballs, footballs, peanuts, or fruit.

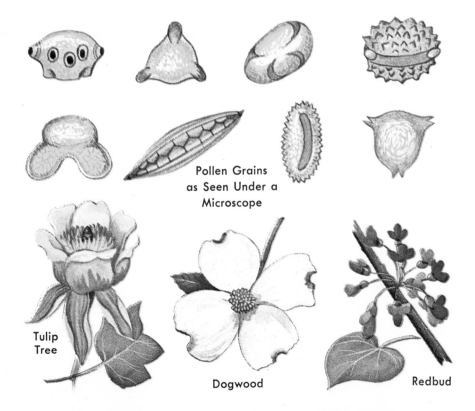

Pollen Grains
as Seen Under a
Microscope

Tulip
Tree

Dogwood

Redbud

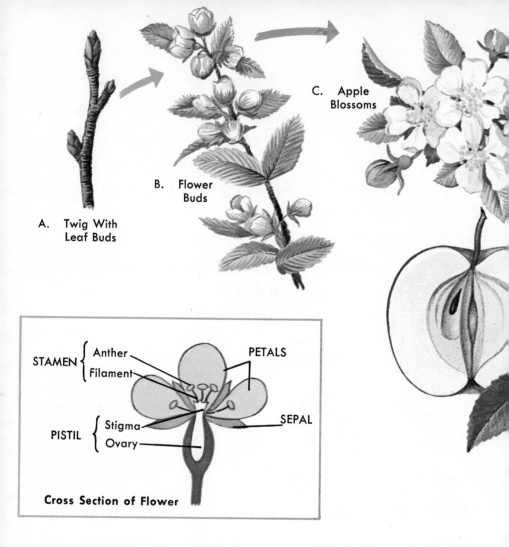

A. **Twig With Leaf Buds**

B. **Flower Buds**

C. **Apple Blossoms**

STAMEN { Anther, Filament }

PETALS

PISTIL { Stigma, Ovary }

SEPAL

Cross Section of Flower

Let's look at an apple blossom to see the part played by pollen in seed production.

The plump base of the flower is the pistil which contains the *ovary*. Five small pointed leaves called *sepals* grow around the pistil, and above them are five pink petals.

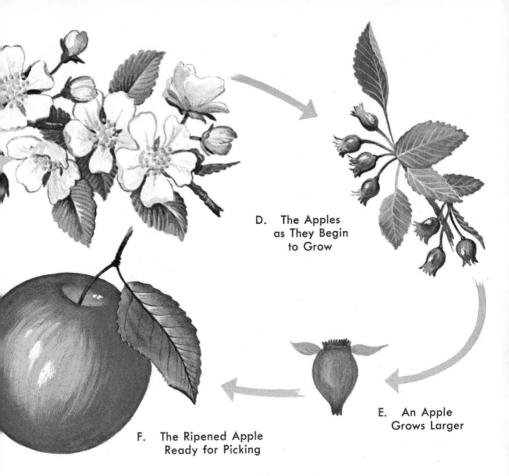

D. The Apples
as They Begin
to Grow

E. An Apple
Grows Larger

F. The Ripened Apple
Ready for Picking

Stamens, which have fine threadlike stalks, grow around the pistil and on the end of each is a thick head. These heads are *anthers* and hold the pollen. The pollen is easily carried to the *stigma*—the tip of the pistil. Each pollen grain then sends down a long tube through the pistil to the ovary. There special cells fertilize the eggs. Each fertilized egg and the tissues around it develops into a seed. The ovary develops into an apple, the fruit.

29

Flowering Trees

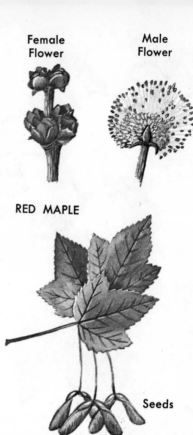

Female Flower   Male Flower

RED MAPLE

Seeds

BOTH THE MALE AND FEMALE flowers grow as separate clusters on red maples. Their seed flowers are a deep, bright red, making the tree a beautiful spring decoration. The male flowers are light pink and yellow. After the seeds are fertilized, the stalks of the female flowers grow long and curve downward. Little spikes push out from the pistils and in a few weeks wing-shaped seeds hang from the branches.

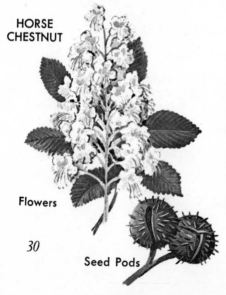

HORSE CHESTNUT

Flowers

Seed Pods

The beautiful white flowers of the horse chestnut form a large spike at the ends of the branches. Only a few flowers of each spike develop into prickly green balls, each containing one to three large, brown seeds.

30

The small, yellow, male flowers of the oak, attached in large numbers along slender stalks, form fingerlike catkins. As the catkins grow they become longer and hang down from the branches like a fringe or string of beads. The female flowers, far fewer in number, are scattered along the branches or are clustered at the tips.

OAK

The river birch has yellow male catkins, opening before or with the leaves. The pollen is carried by the wind to the female catkins.

RIVER BIRCH

The fragrant white flowers of the black locust bloom in long clusters before the leaves are fully grown.

BLACK LOCUST

31

How Seeds Travel

EVERY SEED CONTAINS A TINY PLANT which lives on the food stored within its cover. When the seed finds a place to grow it bursts open the cover and pushes its root into the soil.

Winged Pine Seed

Seed Takes Root

Young Plant

Nature has provided many ways for seeds to travel. The wind is one of their best helpers. The wings on the elm and maple seeds carry them easily through the air on a windy day. The seed balls of sycamores have hairy tufts which help them sail through the air.

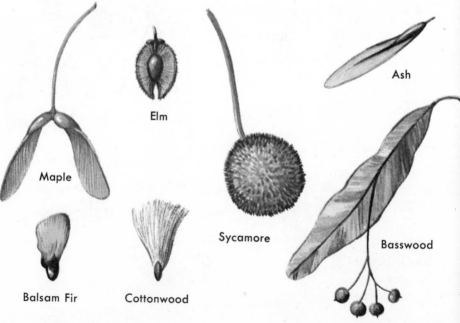

Elm

Ash

Maple

Sycamore

Basswood

Balsam Fir

Cottonwood

Birds help seeds to travel by eating fruit and dropping the seeds in distant places.

Squirrels bury acorns, hickory nuts, and walnuts for winter food, but they do not always find them again. In this way, new trees begin to grow the next spring.

Seeds often fall upon streams and lakes and float to other shores.

They are also carried by people on their clothes as well as being planted by them in specific places.

Our National Forests

EVEN THOUGH MOST OF OUR ORIGINAL FORESTS were destroyed by the pioneers and later by fire, we still have great areas of woodland. There are about one hundred and fifty national forests covering more than 180 million acres. Most of these are in the western states and have been set aside by our government for special purposes. One important purpose is the production of timber. The western forests provide more than half the big timber used for lumber. Another aim is the protection of watersheds. Forested slopes catch the rain and snow. They pour the water gently into streams and rivers and on into the water systems of our homes. The forests in the state of Washington gather and deliver water to more than ten million people. There are also thousands of acres of farm land and orchards irrigated with the snow and rain gathered by national forests. The forests also hold topsoil in place and prevent floods.

In most forests several kinds of trees grow side by side. Oaks live in the cool climate of the Rockies and in the hot Southwest. Some thrive best where there is moisture, but others also grow in dry places and on rocky ridges. Pine, hickory, and oak trees are found growing in the same forests in the southeastern and southern states.

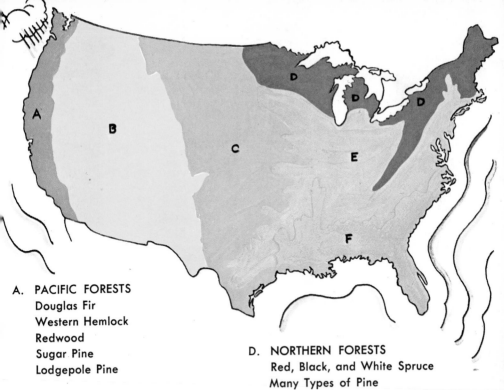

A. PACIFIC FORESTS
Douglas Fir
Western Hemlock
Redwood
Sugar Pine
Lodgepole Pine

B. ROCKY MOUNTAIN FORESTS
Many Types of Pine
Western Red Cedar
Western Hemlock
Douglas Fir

C. PLAINS, PRAIRIE
Trees which grow here were brought
in from other areas and planted.

D. NORTHERN FORESTS
Red, Black, and White Spruce
Many Types of Pine
Maple, Oak, Birch, Aspen, Beech

E. CENTRAL HARDWOOD FORESTS
Oak, Hickory, Ash
Elm, Maple, Cottonwood, Poplar

F. SOUTHERN FORESTS
Slash, Shortleaf, and Longleaf Pine
Southern Oak, Southern Cypress
Red Cedar

There are trees that need a specific climate. The black spruce needs the cool weather and damp soil of the North. The rocky, sandy soil of the far West is the home of the junipers. The black gum grows only in wet, warm sections of the South.

35

Short and Tall

ALL TREES in a forest do not have the same amount of growth. There are those that naturally grow very high, need sunlight, and in some instances are the oldest. In between these tallest trees are shorter ones—those that by nature do not grow extremely tall, and others that are only partly grown. There are also among them some that need shade in order to thrive and others that are hindered from growing by the lack of sunlight. The lowest growth consists of saplings, shrubs, and small plants.

Climate

Trees purify the air we breathe by giving off oxygen from their leaves. They also give off moisture in the form of vapor. One forest gives off thousands of gallons of moisture on a hot day. The vapor keeps the forest cool. It also affects the temperature of the surrounding area.

The vapor from forests rises, adding moisture to the clouds above them. Winds carry these tree clouds great distances. They are an important source of rain for inland states. Ocean clouds cannot get to the prairies because of the cool, mountain air. Without the tree clouds, that region would often suffer because of the lack of rain.

Softwood

Trees furnish us with hundreds of useful products. One of the most useful is lumber, more than half of which is cut from softwood trees—spruce, balsam, pine, and fir.

The Douglas firs are the most valuable for this purpose. They are our second largest trees, some growing two hundred and fifty feet tall and from four to eight feet thick. They grow in our western forests and some live to be three and four hundred years old. The wood is a brownish red and has very few knots. It can be sawed into thick

boards and can also be peeled into thin sheets which are glued together to make plywood.

Much of the strong timber used for fencing, railroad ties, and construction comes from ponderosa pines, also called western yellow pines. These trees live to be very old, too, and become more beautiful with age. Their dull dark brown bark changes to shades of orange and dark red as the years pass, making them the loveliest in the forest.

Southern yellow pines grow in great quantities, therefore produce a large amount of needed lumber. About one third of all the softwood cut in the United States comes from them. Of these pines, the shortleaf, longleaf, slash, and loblolly are the most important.

39

Hardwood

Only a small amount of the lumber used is hardwood, the oaks furnishing a large part of it. There are more species of oaks than any other tree—about seventy in the United States, most growing in the eastern section. Almost all are tall, strong, and majestic, and live for hundreds of years. The white and red oaks are the most common and their wood is used for flooring, furniture, and boats.

The ash, walnut, and hickory trees are also hardwoods. The light brown, sturdy wood of the white ash and the red ash is suitable for tool handles, baseball bats, and hockey sticks.

A Few of the Many Objects Made from Hardwood

Wood for Fuel

NEXT IN QUANTITY USED is wood for fuel. Firewood is still used in millions of homes for heat and for cooking. Some of the best trees for fuel are elm, oak, maple, and black locust. Of these, the black locust is a favorite. A cord of it will burn almost as long as a ton of coal. Other popular firewoods are birch and hickory. Wood is also used in the manufacture of wood alcohol for liquid fuel, and charcoal.

41

A. Logs are carried into the mill.

C. Paper is formed on a paper machine.

Paper

MILLIONS OF TONS OF PAPER are used every year, and the wood pulp from which it is made comes from trees. Most of it comes from the softwoods. A very small number of hardwood trees are used, of which the poplar is the most satisfactory.

The white spruce is the most perfect for wood pulp, as it contains very little resin and its fibers are the right quality.

B. They are crushed and washed.

D. Sometimes a shiny finish is put on the paper.

The wood is ground or treated with chemicals to separate the fibers, forming pulp. Further chemical treatment removes practically all other substances from the cellulose. The fibers are then suitable for making white paper.

The need for these conifers of our northern forests is greater than the supply. Large quantities of spruce-wood pulp and logs are imported from Canada and Europe.

Wonders From Wood

A GREAT AMOUNT OF OUR CLOTHING is made of rayon. This material is also made from the cellulose of trees. Chemicals are used to make the cellulose into a jelly which is then shaped into thin, silklike threads. Cellophane, camera films, and plastics are made from this jelly, too.

In making these products, spruce, fir, western hemlock, aspen, and birch are the most valuable trees. The western hemlocks grow in the Rocky Mountain and northwestern forests. They are extremely tall, and they have narrow, grooved needles and reddish-brown cones.

HEMLOCK

What Tannin
Does for Us

Library Paste
and Woodburgers

HEMLOCKS ALSO GIVE US tannin, a chemical important in the shrinking and softening of leather. Tannin also comes from the bark of the oak, sumac, and chestnut. The chestnut has this acid in both the bark and wood. It was once the main source of tannin, but practically all the trees have been killed by a disease called chestnut blight. Trees that have tannin in their bark are protected by it from damage that might be done to them by some insects.

This chemical is sometimes used in medicines and in the dyeing of materials.

45

Paint From Trees

Paste From Trees

Turpentine and rosin are valuable chemicals produced from the gum of the longleaf and slash pines. Oleoresin, the soft gumlike substance, is drained from the trees by making small cuts into their wood. It can be taken from them year after year without doing them much harm, and comes from stumps as well as living trees. The gum is more plentiful in southern pines, due to their having more tubes which manufacture it.

The gum is processed into turpentine and rosin which are used in paints, varnishes, sealing wax, and synthetic rubber.

Sweet gum trees yield storax, a substance used in library paste, some salves, and in perfuming soaps.

Tall oil is a by-product obtained when paper is made from the wood of resinous trees, such as the southern yellow pine. It is changed by chemical treatments into many useful materials such as drying oil used in manufacturing paint and varnish.

SOUTHERN
YELLOW
PINE

WITCH
HAZEL

Twig

Flower

Witch hazel, which is obtained from the small twigs of the witch hazel tree, is used in some skin lotions. The witch hazel is a strange tree; its flowers bloom in autumn after the leaves fall!

47

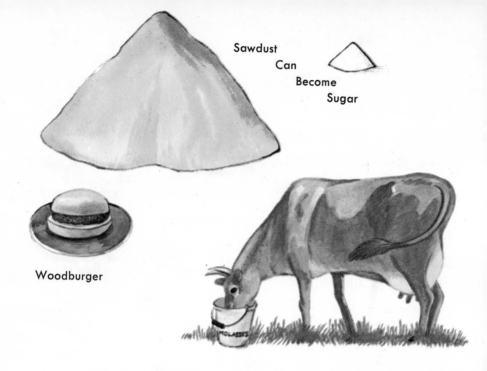

Sawdust Can Become Sugar

Woodburger

Perhaps the greatest miracle of all is that wood can give us food. Scientists are able to change a ton of sawdust into a half ton of sugar. The sugar is not as pleasant to eat as that made from maple sap, but it is most valuable. It can be used to grow torula yeast which contains all the properties of meat protein. "Woodburgers" were eaten by some people in Europe during a meat shortage in World War II.

A ton of dry wood can also be changed into 180 gallons of molasses. This is used as a basic food for cattle.

And even the bark and leaves are made into useful products. Bark is used in insulation materials. Leaves are ground into mulch for earth coverings to hold moisture.

Fruit

FRUIT TREES FALL INTO TWO GROUPS—those that grow wild, and those that are cultivated. The apples, cherries, peaches, pears, and plums that are bought in markets come from orchards that have been planted for that purpose. The citrus groves of southern California and Florida are also grown for commercial use. From them we get oranges, lemons, limes, and grapefruit. There are more oranges and apples in cultivation than any other fruits.

The wild fruits, such as crab apples, cherries, persimmons and mulberries are not usually eaten by humans. Their blossoms—except for the mulberry which has no conspicuous flower—add to the beauty of the woodlands and their fruit provides food for wildlife.

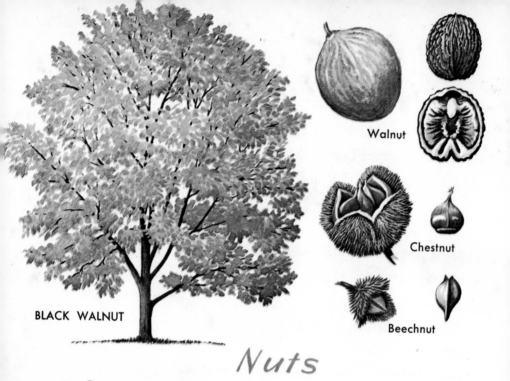

Walnut

Chestnut

Beechnut

BLACK WALNUT

Nuts

Some forest trees are called "nut" trees because their seeds are a valuable food. Of these, pecans and walnuts are the most popular. Pecan trees grow wild in the Mississippi Valley and the southern states. In order to supply the demand for the nuts, huge groves have been planted.

The sturdy black walnut tree grows across the eastern half of the United States. The nut shells are covered with a thick green husk which dries, turns brown, and shreds apart when the nuts are ripe.

Chestnuts grow inside a covering of sharp burrs.

Beech seeds are protected by a burrlike case. Inside this case is a shell, and inside the shell are two or three seeds.

50

The Largest Trees

THE GIANT REDWOOD TREES of California are the largest in the world. They are the sequoia species of conifers and grow from 200 to 340 feet tall. Their needles and cones are only about an inch long, and the cones have very few seeds. These redwoods have no taproots, but their thousands of smaller roots spread over a wide area. New shoots spring up from some of them and begin growing into young trees. The tallest of the redwoods is 364 feet high and is named the Founders Tree.

Another type of sequoia is known as big tree. One of these is named the General Sherman and is 101½ feet in circumference, and 272 feet high. This marvelous tree is more than 3,800 years old.

Unusual Trees

THE DWARF JUNIPER is a strange little tree that grows in almost every part of the United States. It is only five to six feet tall—not much taller than a bush. Although it is an evergreen, it has berries instead of cones. The blue berries have a waxy coating and their fragrance attracts birds.

Some people consider the Joshua tree to be the ugliest in existence. The stumpy branches come from the top of the tree and turn and twist in odd ways. At the very ends of the branches there are bunches of bristly needles. The blossoms are a pale, greenish white and their pollen is carried by a white moth.

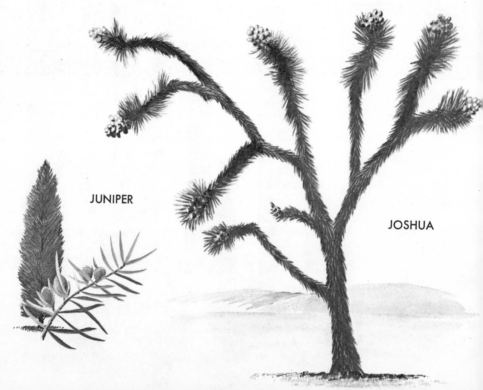

JUNIPER

JOSHUA

Trees Have Enemies

THROUGH THE AGES trees have had to combat many enemies. Man, in his destructiveness, has been their worst foe. Fires, often started by careless people, have destroyed thousands upon thousands of forest acres. A campfire left burning or a lighted match thoughtlessly thrown into the woods can cause the loss of millions of dollars' worth of trees and their valuable products.

Whole forests are lost by fire.

Wind damages some trees.

Wasteful cutting has also taken a heavy toll. From the time of the early settlers, forests have been felled without thought as to the future supply of wood.

Like humans, trees have to struggle against climate and disease. Strong winds, lack of moisture, or sudden cold temperature can cause them to die.

They are plagued by many infections. Bleeding canker is a disease of the sugar maple. It causes the bark to crack. At times a liquid seeps through which when dry resembles blood.

Some insects are vicious enemies. Bark beetles lay their eggs beneath the hard bark and the larvae feed upon the soft bark and cambium.

Mistletoe is a plant that damages trees by obtaining water and some of its food from the tree.

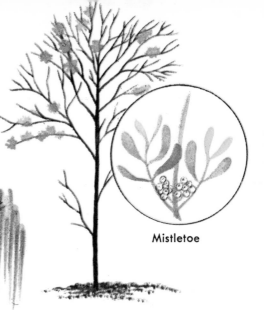

Mistletoe

Live oaks are often smothered by Spanish moss that hangs like a fringe from their branches.

Spanish Moss

Animals damage trees, too.

And too, rabbits and porcupines injure trees by gnawing the bark, and beavers fell them to build dams.

Trees Have Friends

NATURE HAS SUPPLIED TREES with friends among which are birds, bats, toads, and some kinds of insects. Of these, the downy woodpeckers are the most helpful as their chief food is the wood-boring ant that harms tree trunks. The hairy woodpeckers also help by eating the eggs of wood-boring beetles.

Ladybug beetles and tree toads feast on millions of lice that suck the leaves.

Forest animals are also friends of trees. They feed on small plants, weeding out the undergrowth that hinders the survival of seedlings.

These Are a
Tree's Friends

Bats

Deer

Woodpeckers

Tree
Frogs

Ladybugs

Protectors of Trees

IN 1905 THE UNITED STATES FOREST SERVICE was organized to protect and increase the number of trees. Lookout towers were built in forests. From them watchmen can spot fires and put them out before great damage is done. Smoke jumpers have been trained to work as paratroopers from airplanes so that fires can be fought more quickly.

The Forest Service has taught lumbermen how to cut trees so as not to harm the rest of the forest. They leave them in places where the wind can scatter seeds and start new forests. Lumbermen also plant new trees to replace those cut and those killed by disease.

Foresters have found better ways of breeding trees by selecting seeds from those that are resistant to disease. Seedlings are planted in special beds. They are watched and tested before being planted in forests.

Tree surgeons are able to repair injured trees in somewhat the same way that dentists fix teeth. They clean out the diseased or injured part

of a tree. Then they fill the cavity, or hole, with tar or cement. This prolongs the life of the tree. They also bolt and brace damaged trees in order to hold them together.

Chemical sprays are used by tree surgeons to kill pests. Asphalt varnish is brushed on tree wounds to help them heal.

Trees are man's priceless friends. Everyone should try to protect them so that they may go on performing their miracles.

59

WHAT IS MOON MILK?

HOW DO ENGINES WORK?

HOW DEEP CAN DIVERS GO?

Whitman
Learn About Books

THE MICROSCOPE AND A HIDDEN WORLD TO EXPLORE *Irene S. Pyszkowski*

Learn how man discovered the hidden world of the invisible. Find out how microscopes are used by detectives, scientists, doctors, and how it is possible to see tiny living things all around us.

ASTRONOMY—OUR SOLAR SYSTEM AND BEYOND *Robert I. Johnson*

Find out about the planets and moons that circle our star, the Sun. Look at actual photographs of craters on the moon, giant tornadoes on the Sun, and exploding stars millions of miles away from us.

ADVENTURES IN SCIENCE *Charles D. Neal*

Experiments to be done at home show how sound, heat, and light travel . . . why lemon juice can be used to write secret messages . . . why a can heated in just the right way crumples when it cools—and much more.

FIND OUT! FIRST STEP TO THE FUTURE *Dr. Dan Q. Posin*

Have you ever wondered how a telescope works? Or how storms happen? Or how the big electronic brains work? Or how atoms join to make all things on Earth—and in space? Dr. Posin has the answers!

ROCKETS TO EXPLORE THE UNKNOWN *Don E. Rogers*

Learn how rockets, and cannons—and bicycles!—are all a little alike. Find out how rockets work, and how they are being designed to fly faster and farther, to carry man out into unknown space.